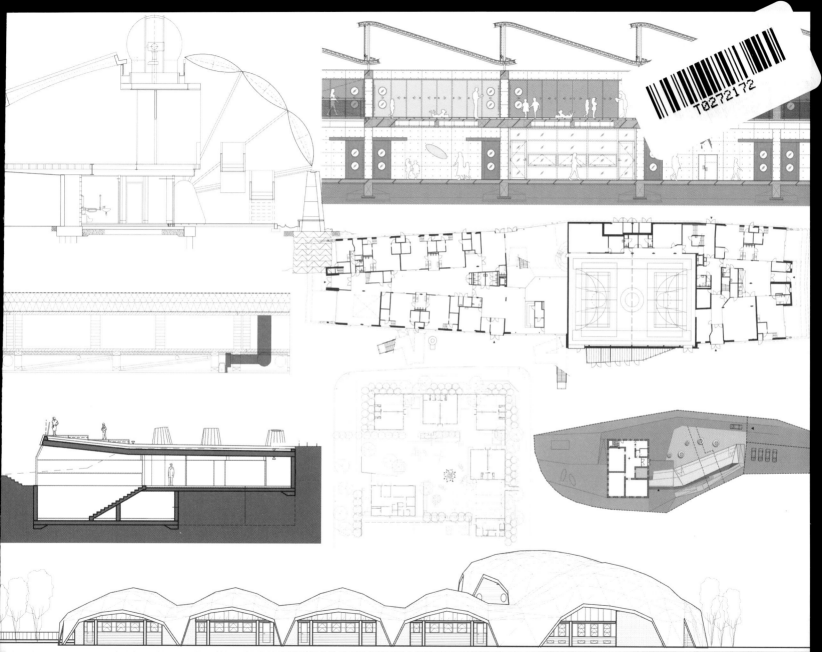

Kindergarten&School
PLANS

© 2021 Instituto Monsa de ediciones.

First edition in April 2021 by Monsa Publications,
Gravina 43 (08930) Sant Adrià de Besós.
Barcelona (Spain) T +34 93 381 00 93
www.monsa.com monsa@monsa.com

Editor and Project Director Anna Minguet
Art director Eva Minguet
(Monsa Publications)
Printing Gómez Aparicio

Shop online:
www.monsashop.com

Follow us!
Instagram: @monsapublications
Facebook: @monsashop

ISBN: 978-84-17557-32-4
D.L. B 4230-2021
April 2021

Kindergarten&School
PLANS

monsa

SCHOOL SPACES SHOULD BE ROOMY, WELL LIT, WELL VENTILATED, WHERE STUDENTS FEEL COMFORTABLE.

Los espacios deben ser amplios, iluminados, con buena ventilación, donde los alumnos se sientan cómodos.

The structures whose designs are included in this publication share the same function: education. This essential function determines each of their features. It reminds us of the importance of the service these buildings provide to society and the need for them to accomplish their function in the best possible way. The concept that education is the basis of all social progress is not new. There is no more important development in society than the education of the individuals who make it up.

Las construcciones cuyos proyectos recoge este volumen comparten una misma razón de ser: la educación. Esta función fundamental determina cada una de sus características, y nos recuerda tanto la importancia del servicio que prestan estos edificios a la sociedad, como la necesidad de que desarrollen su labor de la mejor manera posible. No es nueva la concepción de que la educación es la base de todo progreso social. No hay evolución más importante en la sociedad que la educación de los individuos que la integran.

SCHOOL FACILITIES SHOULD EVOLVE OVER TIME AND SHOULD ALWAYS BE APPROPRIATE TO THE AGE OF THE STUDENTS.

Las instalaciones de la escuela se deben ir modificando con el paso del tiempo y estar siempre acordes a las edades de los alumnos.

This is why the architectural design of educational centers and, in particular, of daycare centers, kindergartens, and schools, is so crucial. This publication illustrates the customization of numerous architectural solutions according to the different stages of pupils' education, from the very youngest up to eighteen years of age, in many different parts of the world.

Por todo ello resulta tan decisivo el desarrollo de la arquitectura de centros educativos y, en particular, de guarderías, jardines de infancia y escuelas. Este volumen ilustra la adaptación de numerosas soluciones arquitectónicas a las distintas etapas de formación de los alumnos, desde la más temprana edad hasta los dieciocho años, en muy distintas partes del mundo.

The projects included in this compilation have been selected because of their success in offering an ideal environment and infrastructure for learning, and because they have been designed to promote coexistence and the exchange of knowledge and ideas. In addition to being a center where knowledge is disseminated, school is a place where people learn to think, share, and live together; hence the importance that projects dedicated to these centers have as many resources and innovations as possible, as well as the most appropriate space conceivable.

Los proyectos incluidos en esta recopilación han sido seleccionados por su acierto a la hora de ofrecer un ambiente y una infraestructura idóneos para el aprendizaje, pero también por haber sido diseñados para promover la convivencia y el intercambio de saberes e inquietudes. La escuela, además de un centro donde se imparten conocimientos, es un lugar donde se aprende a pensar, a compartir y a convivir; de ahí la importancia de que los proyectos dedicados a estos centros cuenten con la mayor cantidad de recursos e innovaciones y con un espacio lo más adecuado posible.

Moreover, schools are no longer just buildings with classrooms. Many of the centers shown in this book also act as meeting places for the community in which they are situated. For example, residents can use the libraries, assembly halls, or sports facilities outside of school hours.

Por otra parte, la escuela ha dejado de ser únicamente un edificio con aulas. Muchos de los centros que muestra este libro funcionan también como espacio de encuentro para la comunidad en que se insertan. Por ejemplo, fuera del horario lectivo, los vecinos pueden hacer uso de sus bibliotecas, salones de actos o instalaciones deportivas.

INFRASTRUCTURE AS A "SMART" TOOL.

La infraestructura como herramienta "inteligente".

Another feature that distinguishes these projects from the classic school concept is their "smart" character. The design of all these buildings shares a common criterion of respect for the environment and a planned layout of their design elements to achieve the greatest possible energy savings. Each one has been designed to offer the best available lighting and natural ventilation.
This publication is a sampling of the most current architectural designs from around the world aimed at stimulating the learning process of students of different ages while ensuring their comfort and safety.

Otro de los aspectos que alejan a estos proyectos de la concepción clásica de la escuela es su carácter "inteligente". El diseño de todos estos edificios comparte un criterio de respeto por el medio ambiente y una planificada disposición de sus elementos para lograr el mayor ahorro de energía posible. Se ha trabajado en cada uno para ofrecer las mejores condiciones de iluminación y ventilación natural.
La presente es una muestra del trabajo más actual de arquitectos de todo el mundo para estimular el proceso de aprendizaje de alumnos de distintas edades, garantizando a su vez aspectos tan importantes como su comodidad y seguridad.

IMPROVE OUTDOOR SPACES BY PLANTING AN ABUNDANCE OF TREES AND HEDGES FOR IMPROVED AIR QUALITY.

Mejorar los espacios exteriores plantando abundantes árboles y setos para favorecer la calidad del aire.

School architecture involves a continuous quest to adapt the different indoor and outdoor spaces for children's play. Interior spaces should be fun when the weather does not allow for going outdoors.
To improve air quality, we recommend that trees and hedges be planted in abundance around the building.

La arquitectura en las escuelas es una continua búsqueda por adaptadar los diferentes espacios interiores y exteriores para sus juegos. Los interiores deben resultar divertidos cuando la climatología no permite salir.
En los exteriores es recomendable para mejorar la calidad del aire, plantar abundantes árboles y setos en torno al edificio.

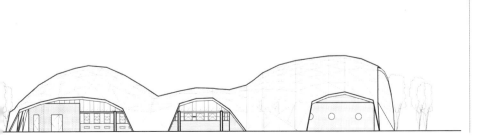

ENERGY SAVING SOLUTIONS.

Soluciones de ahorro energético.

Various energy-saving solutions are available, including a low-condensing boiler, photoelectric controls for exterior lighting, and a rainwater drainage system.

Existen distintas soluciones de ahorro energético, entre las que destacan la caldera de baja condensación, los controles fotoeléctricos para la iluminación exterior y sistemas de drenaje de agua de lluvia.

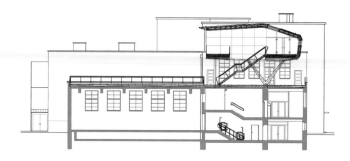
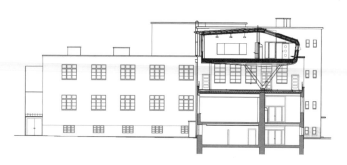

THE IMPORTANCE THAT COLOR CAN PLAY IN THE CLASSROOM.

La importancia que puede tener el color en las aulas.

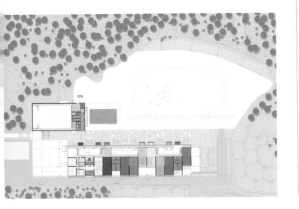

Color plays a crucial role in creating an environment that fosters learning.
Using the right color, or knowing the right combination of colors, can significantly benefit emotions, attention, and the development of creativity.
The use of green to enhance concentration and relaxation, orange to stimulate the mind, or blue to enhance students' cognitive processes are just a few examples.

El color juega un papel clave en la creación de un entorno que fomente el aprendizaje.
Utilizar el color adecuado, o saber la combinación correcta puede beneficiar en gran medida las emociones, la atención y el desarrollo de la creatividad.
El uso del color verde para potenciar la concentración y la relajación, el color naranja para estimular la mente, o el color azul para potenciar los procesos cognitivos del alumnado son solo algunos ejemplos.

INDEX

KASTELLET SCHOOL

DIV. A ARKITEKTER
Location: Oslo, Norway
Photos: © DIV. A Arkitekter, Jiri Havran

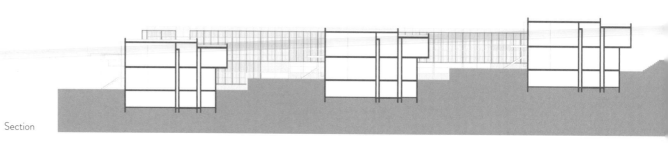

Section

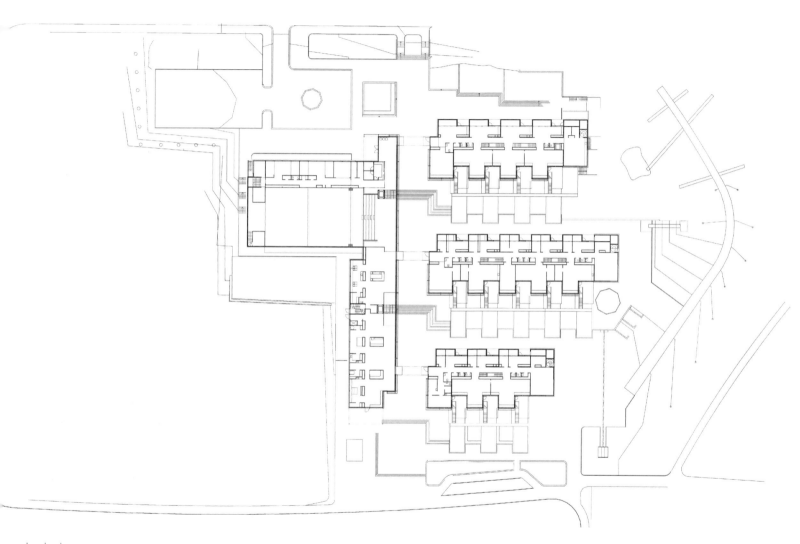

Low level

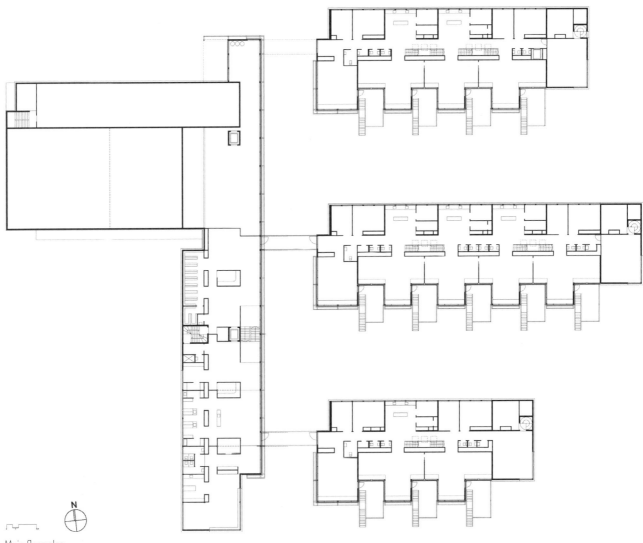

Main floor plan

THE PUIET

ARTEKS ARCHITECTS

Location: Ordino, Andorra
Photos: © Eugeni Pons

North elevation

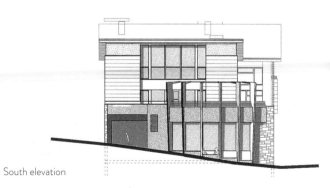

South elevation

East elevation

West elevation

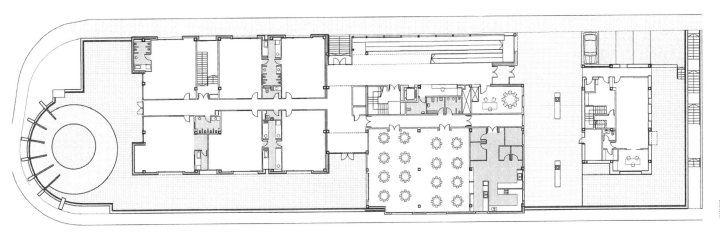

First floor plan

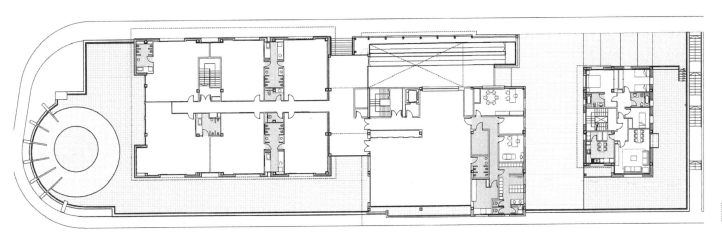

Second floor plan

NDNA REGIONAL CENTER

COTTRELL & VERMEULEN ARCHITECTURE

Location: London, UK
Photos: © Peter Grant

Site plan

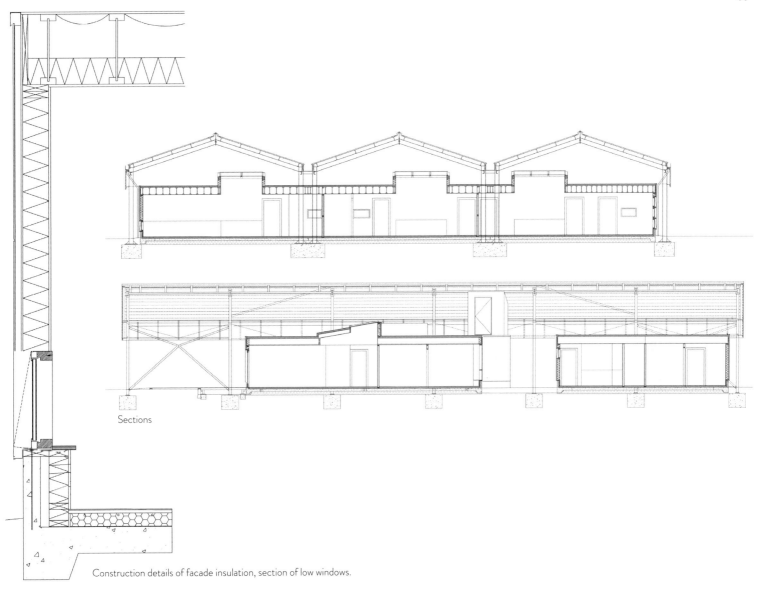

Sections

Construction details of facade insulation, section of low windows.

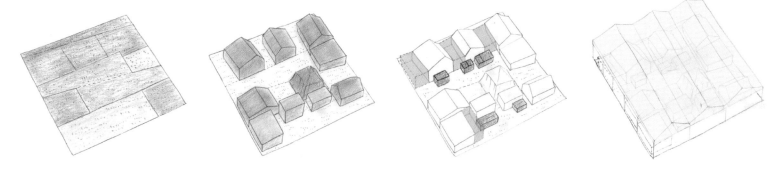

Sketch

3D sketch

PRIMARY SCHOOL IN BABYLON

GRUZEN SAMTON ARCHITECTS

Location: New York, USA
Photos: © John Woodruff, Peter Brown

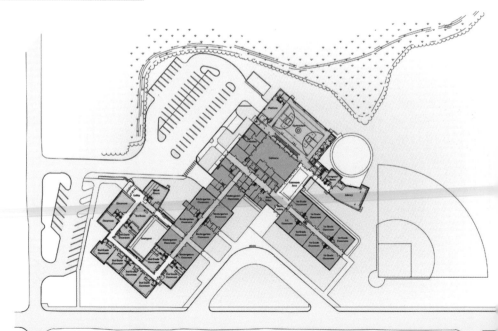

Site plan

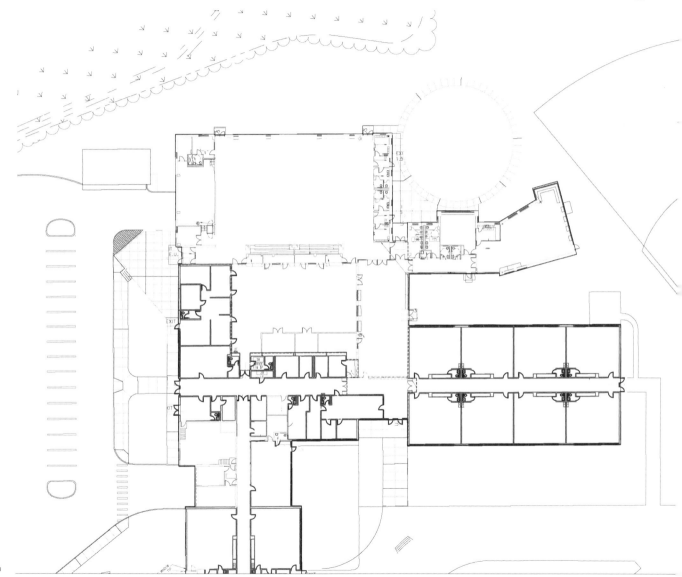

Main floor plan

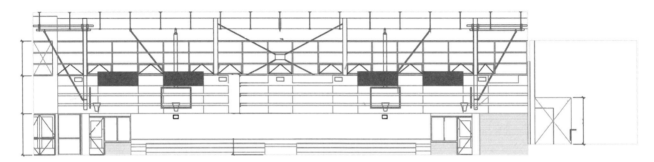

West elevation

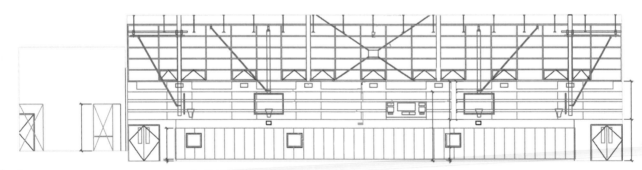

East elevation

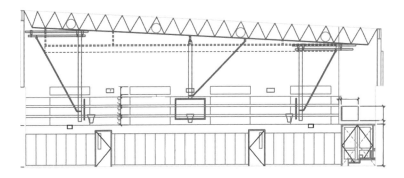

South elevation

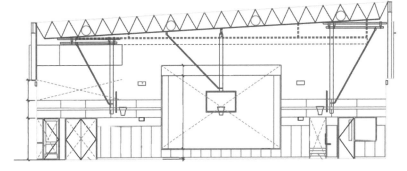

North elevation

LAUSD ELEMENTARY CENTER

RIOS CLEMENTI HALE STUDIOS

Location: Los Angeles, USA

Photos: © Tom Bonner

Site plan

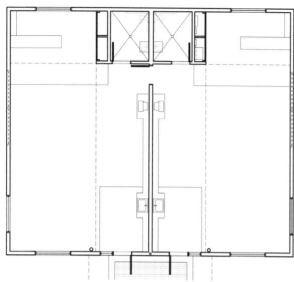

Section AA

Main floor plan

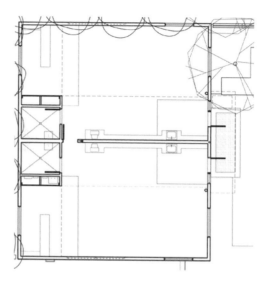

Section BB

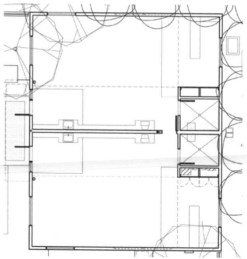

Section CC

ASTRONOMY CLASS

STUDIO E ARCHITECTS

Location: North Kensington, UK
Photos: © Marie Louise Halpenny, Studio E Architects

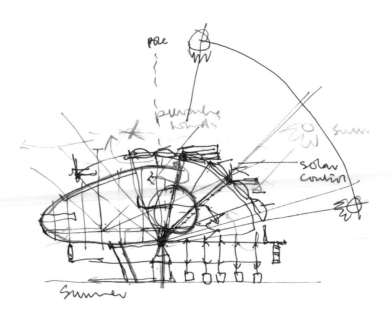

Sketch

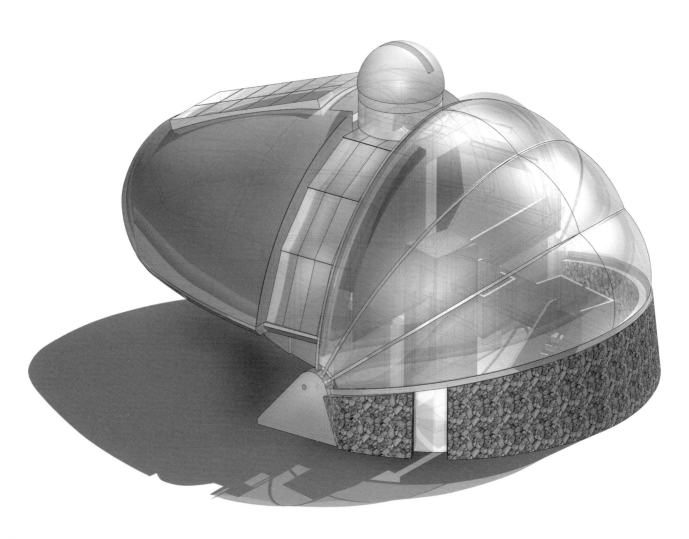

3D sketch

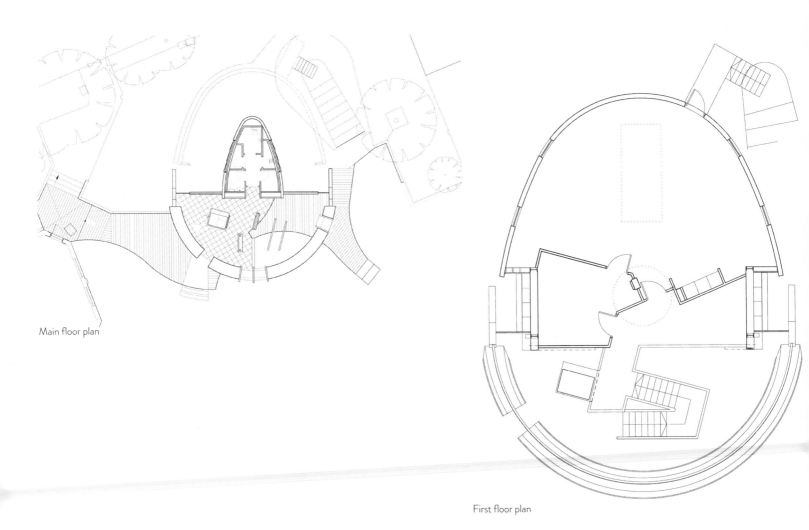

Main floor plan

First floor plan

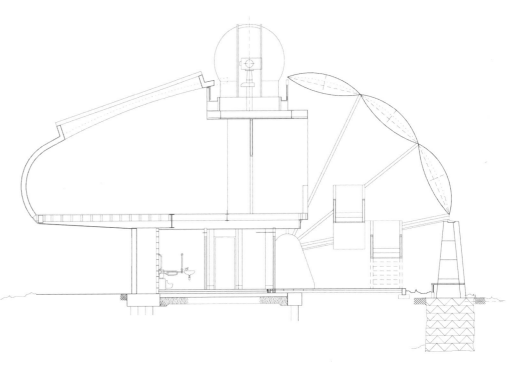

Section

KINDERGARTEN IN EGG

DIETRICH UNTERTRIFALLER

Location: Egg, Austria
Photos: © Bruno Klomfar

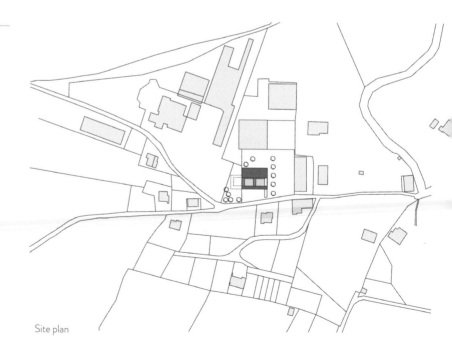

Site plan

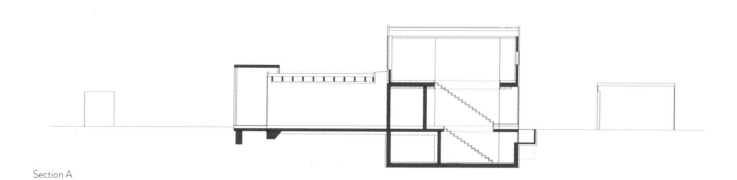

Section A

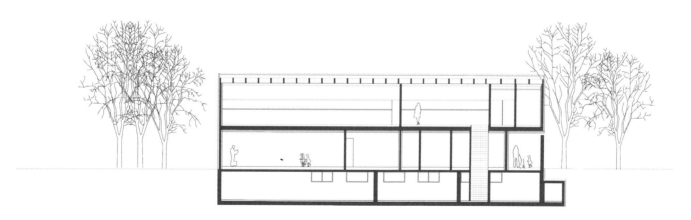

Section B

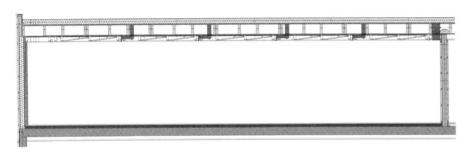

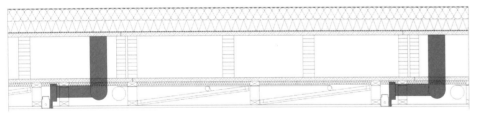

Roof section

BREDE SCHOOL

VENHOEVEN ARCHITECTS
Location: Utrecht, Netherlands
Photos: © Luuk Kramer

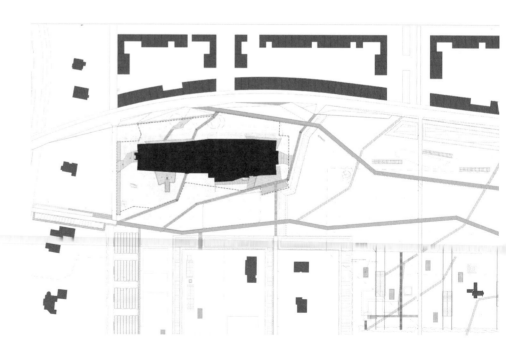

Site plan

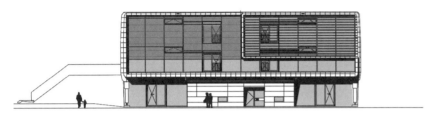

East elevation

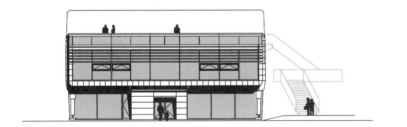

West elevation

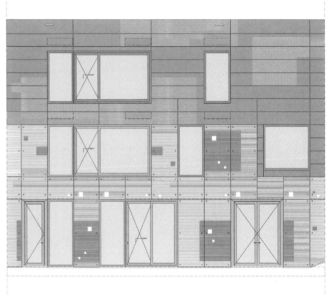

East section

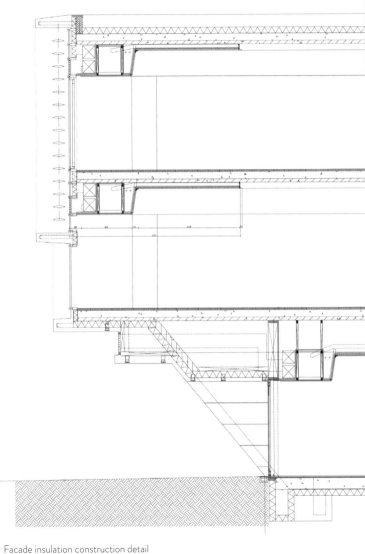

Facade insulation construction detail

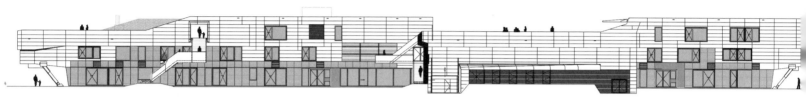

West elevation facade

North elevation facade

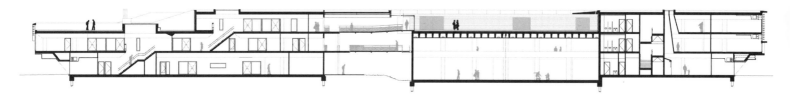

West elevation

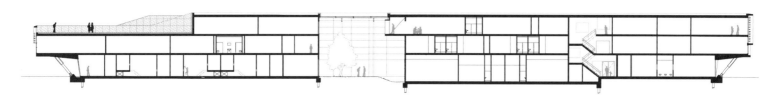

North elevation

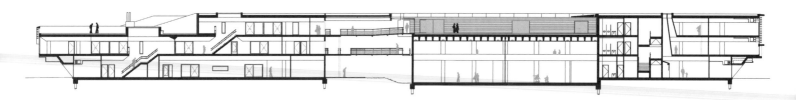

East elevation

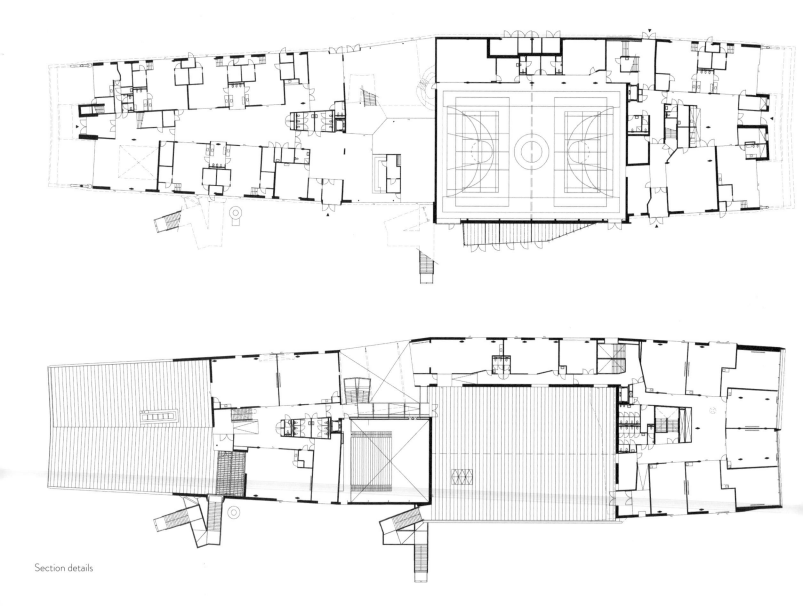

Section details

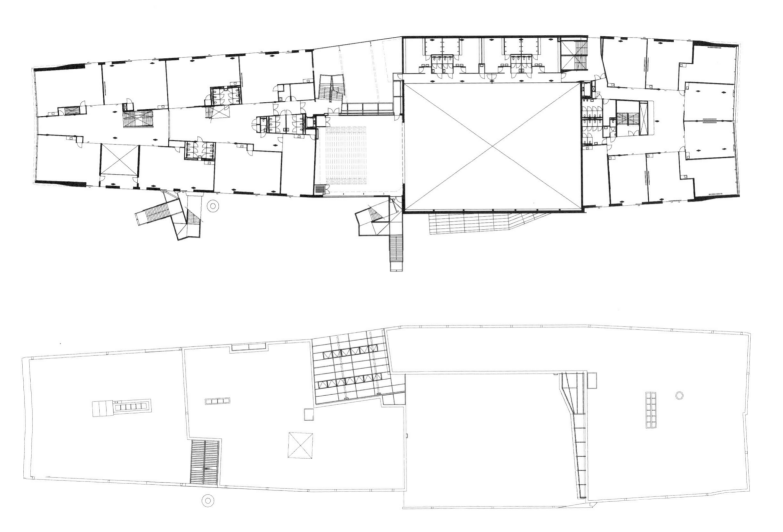

Section details

NATORPGASSE SCHOOL

ANDREAS TREUSCH

Location: Viena, Austria

Photos: © Rupert Steiner

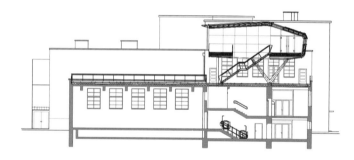

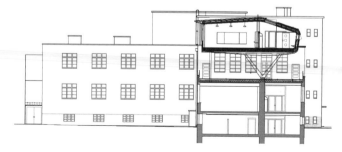

Sections

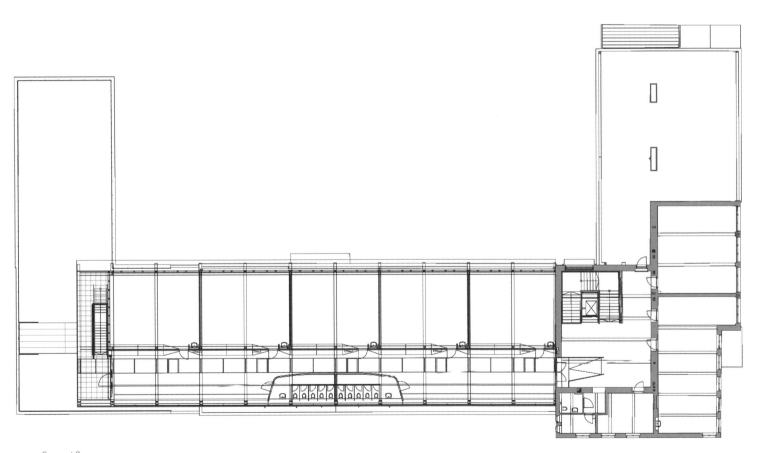

Second floor

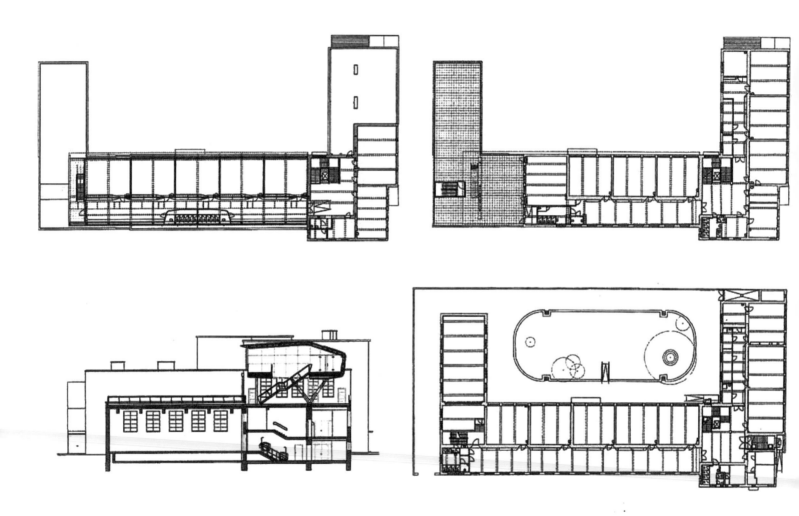

Sections

KINDERGARTEN ARCOBALENO

FABIO DELLA TORRE, BIGI

Location: Morbegno, Italy
Photos: © Andrea Martiradonna

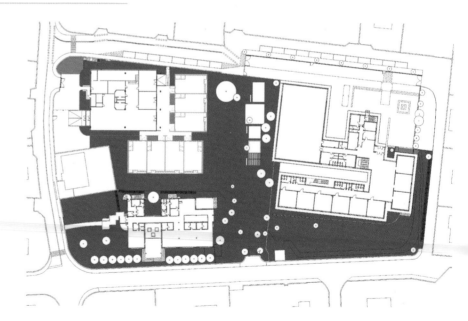

Site plan

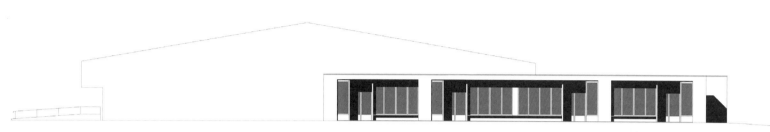

Section

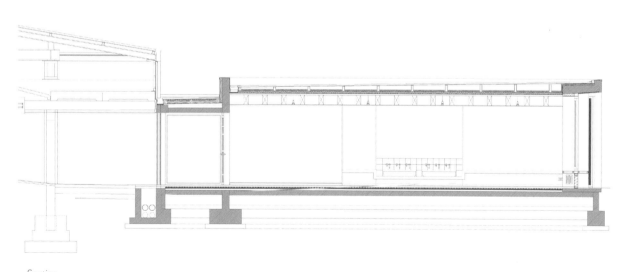

Section

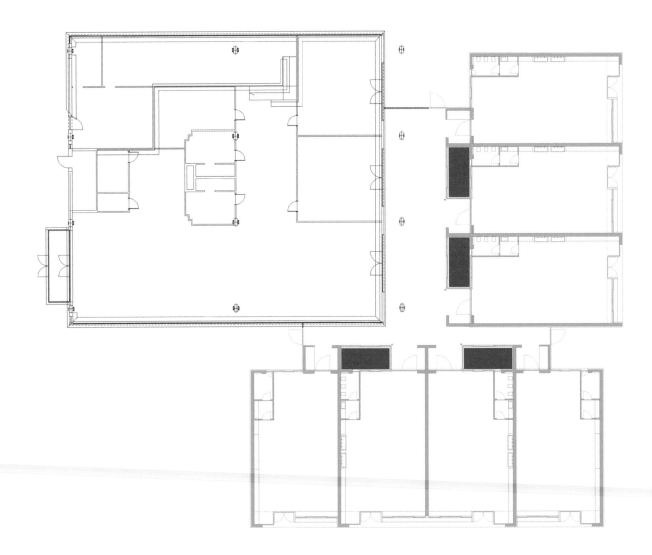

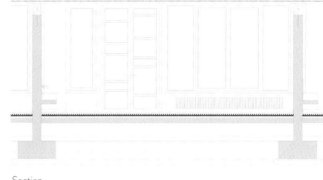

Section

Section detail

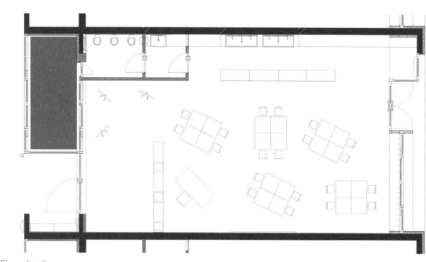

Floor detail

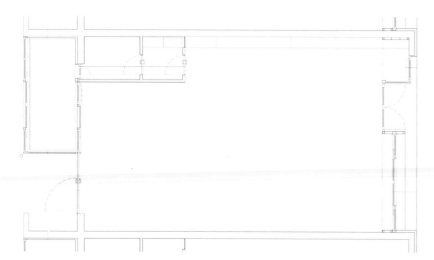

Section details

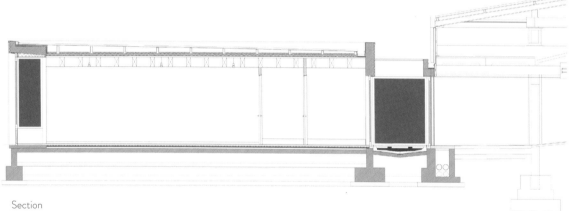

Section

SÃO PAULO SCHOOL

MARCOS ACAYABA

Location: São Paulo Brazil

Photos: © Nelson Kon, Gal Oppido (FDE archive)

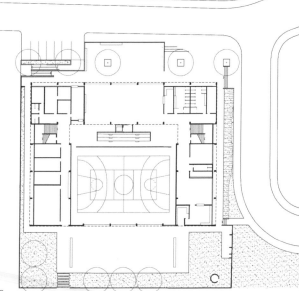

Main floor plan

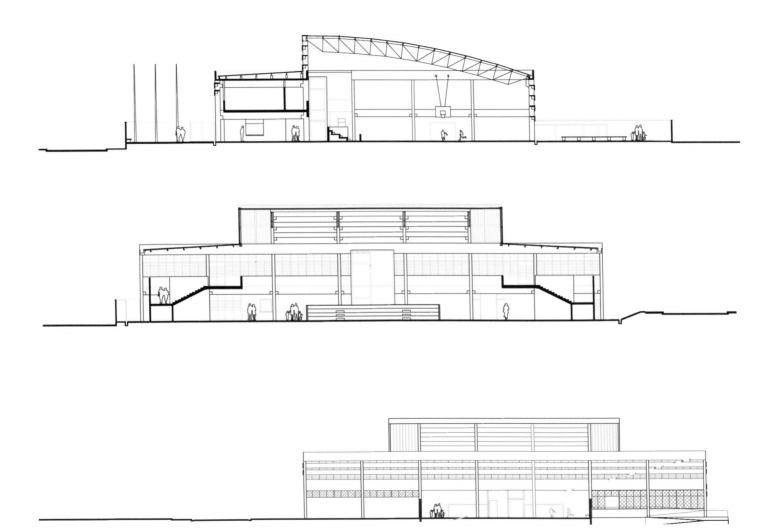

Sections

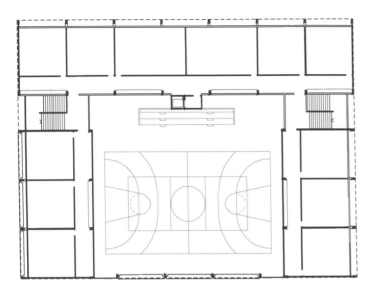

Floor plan

RAFAEL AROZARENA SECONDARY INSTITUTE

AMP ARCHITECTS
Location: Tenerife, Spain
Photos: © Miguel de Guzmán

Site plan

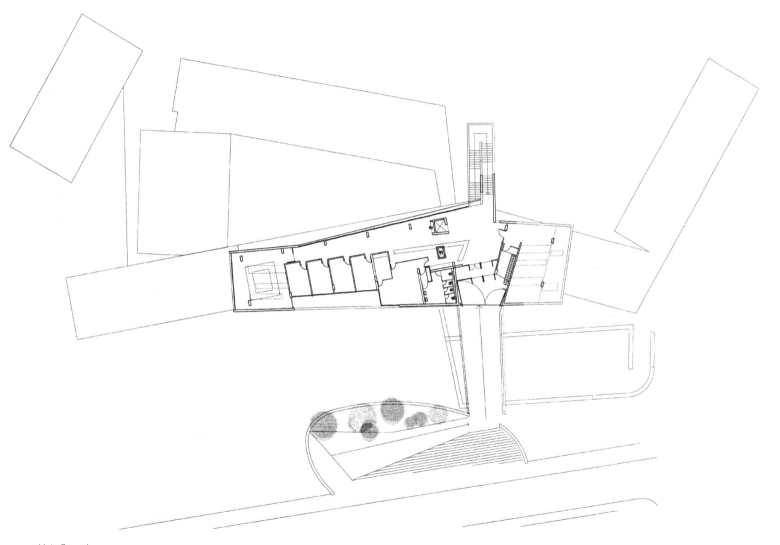

Main floor plan

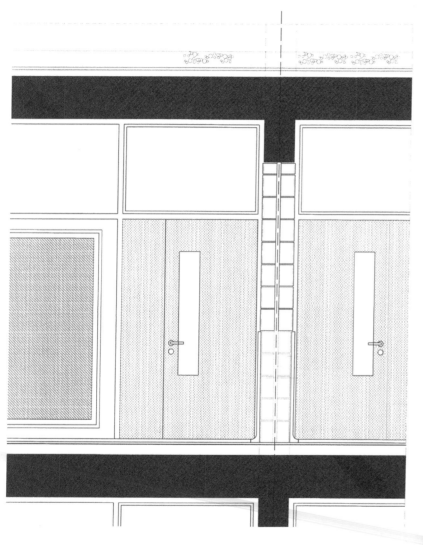

Classroom detail

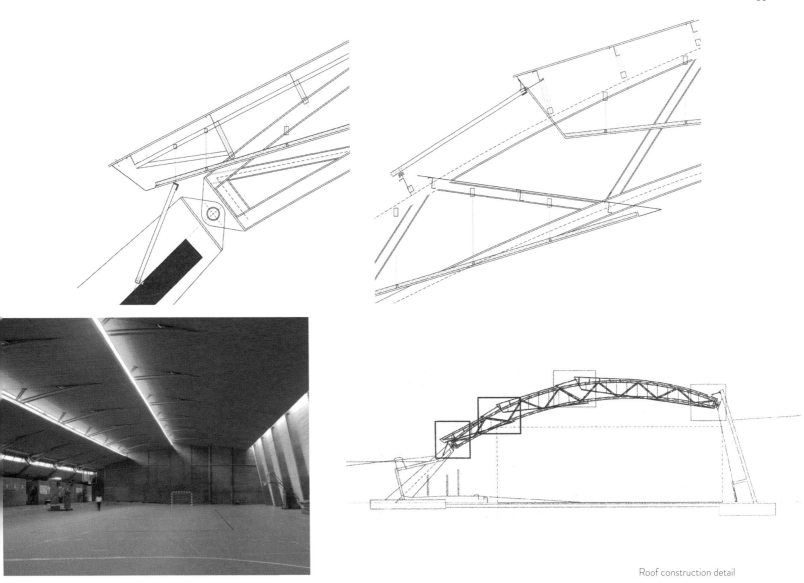

Roof construction detail

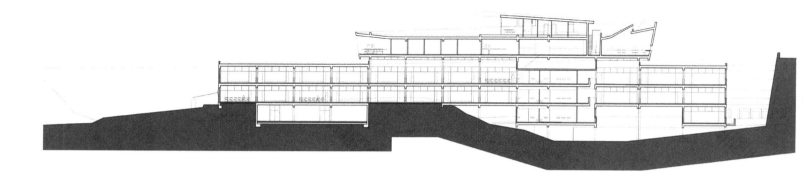

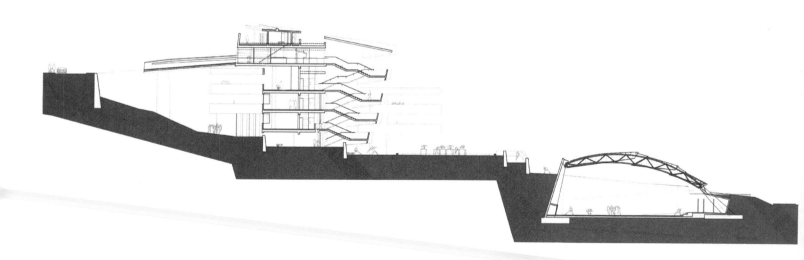

Sections

MUSIC SCHOOL IN GRATKORN

WINKLER ARCHITEKTUR
Location: Styria, Austria
Photos: © Paul Ott

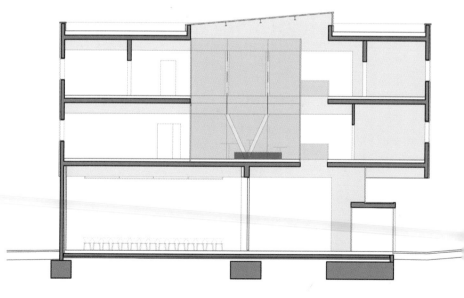

Section

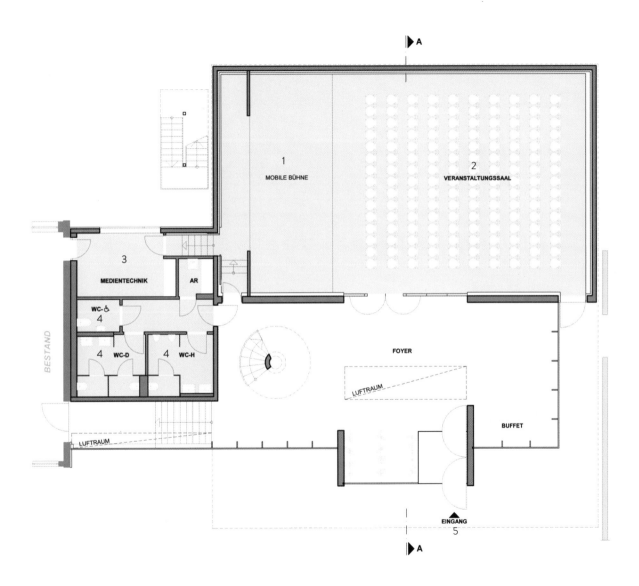

A

1
MOBILE BÜHNE

2
VERANSTALTUNGSSAAL

3
MEDIENTECHNIK

AR

WC-♿
4

4   WC-D

4   WC-H

BESTAND

FOYER

LUFTRAUM

LUFTRAUM

BUFFET

EINGANG

5

A

Ground floor plan
1. Mobile stage
2. Event hall
3. Media technology
4. WC
5. Entrance

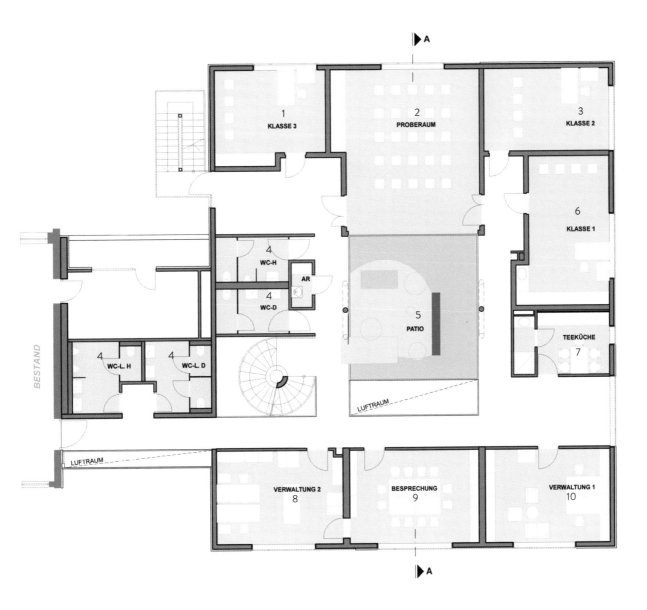

A

1
KLASSE 3

2
PROBERAUM

3
KLASSE 2

6
KLASSE 1

4
WC-H

AR

4
WC-D

4
WC-L. H

4
WC-L. D

5
PATIO

TEEKÜCHE
7

LUFTRAUM

BESTAND

LUFTRAUM

VERWALTUNG 2
8

BESPRECHUNG
9

VERWALTUNG 1
10

A

Main floor plan
1. Class 3
2. Rehearsal room
3. Class 2
4. WC
5. Patio
6. Class 1
7. Kitchen
8. Administration 2
9. Meeting
10. Administration 1

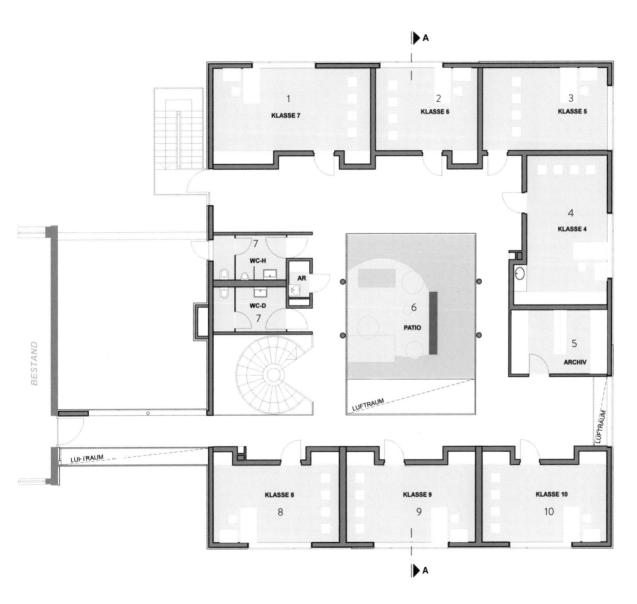

BESTAND

1
KLASSE 7

2
KLASSE 6

3
KLASSE 5

4
KLASSE 4

7
WC-H

AR

WC-D

7

6
PATIO

5
ARCHIV

LUFTRAUM

LUFTRAUM

LUFTRAUM

8
KLASSE 8

9
KLASSE 9

10
KLASSE 10

A

A

Second floor plan
1. Class 7
2. Class 6
3. Class 5
4. Class 4
5. Archive
6. Patio
7. WC
8. Class 8
9. Class 9
10. Class 10

KINDERGARTEN IN LEISACH

MACHNÉ ARCHITEKTEN

Location: Lienz, Austria
Photos: © Paul Ott

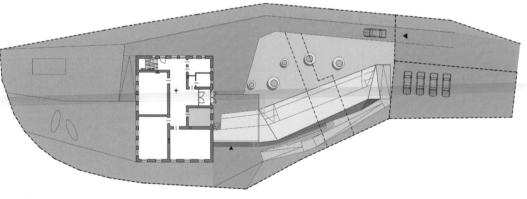

Site plan

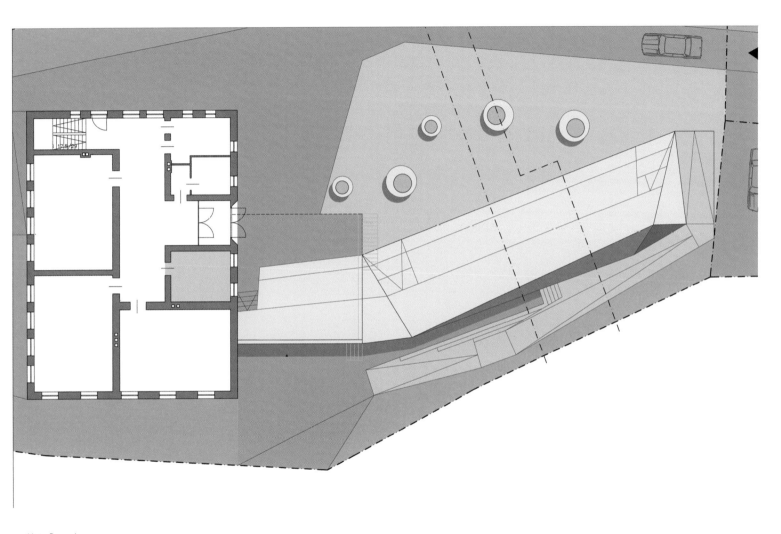

Main floor plan

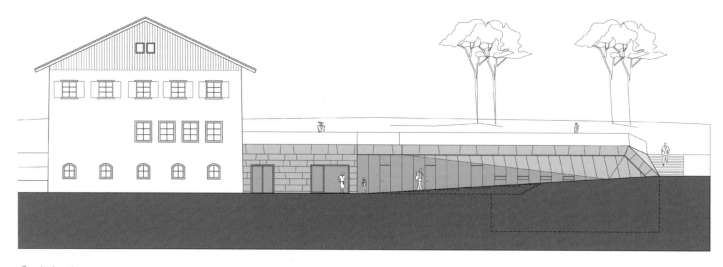

South elevation

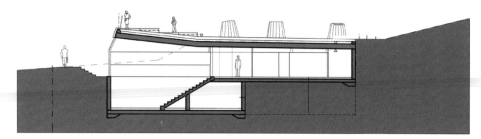

Section

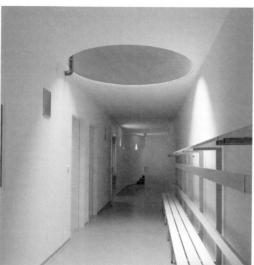

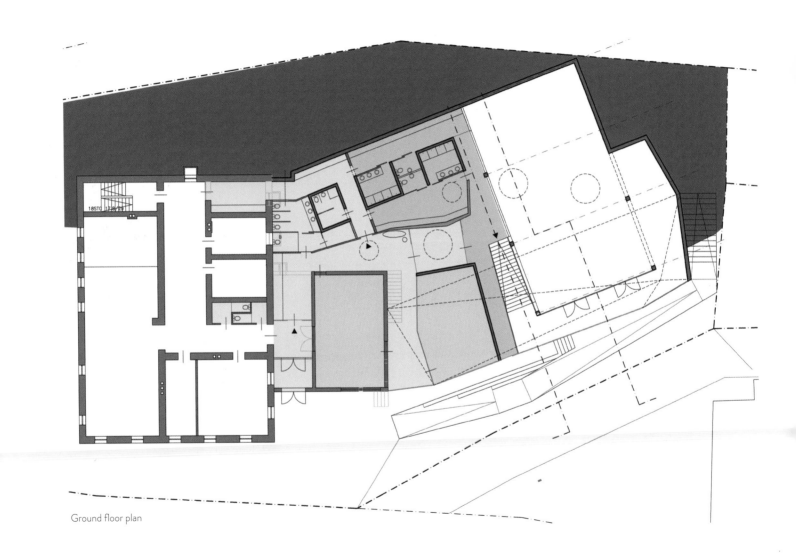

Ground floor plan

BUBBLETECTURE

SHUHEI ENDO
Location: Shiga, Japan
Photos: © Yoshiharu Matsumura

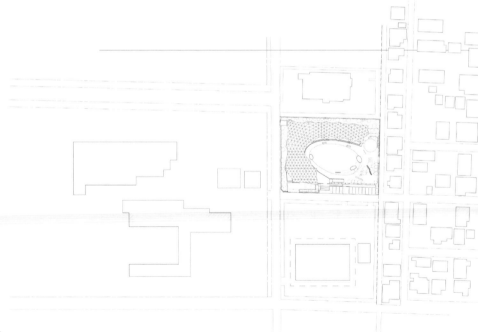

Main floor plan

West elevation

South elevation

East elevation

North elevation

Section A

Section B

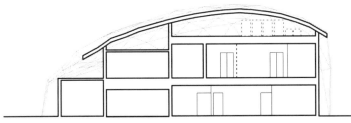

Section C

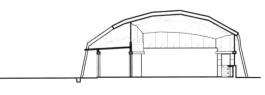

Classroom section

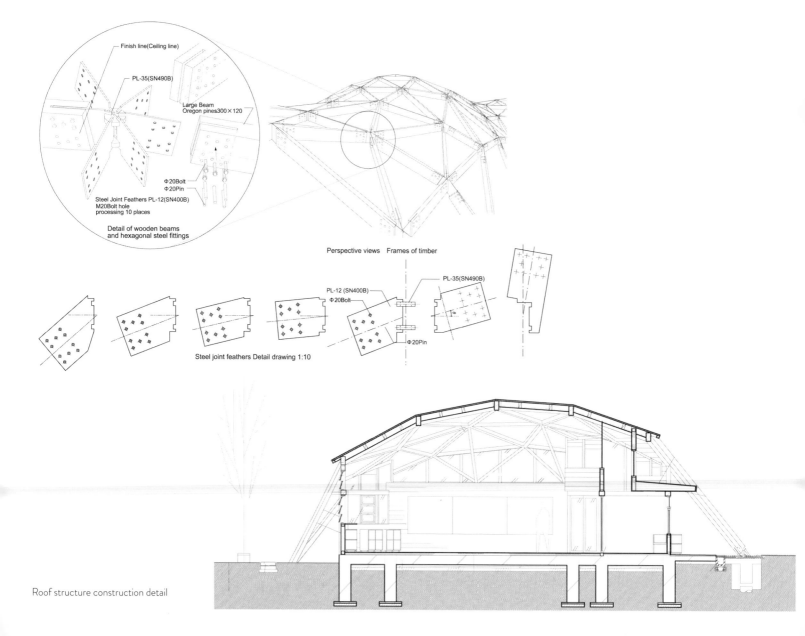

Finish line(Ceiling line)

PL-35(SN490B)

Large Beam
Oregon pines300×120

Φ20Bolt
Φ20Pin

Steel Joint Feathers PL-12(SN400B)
M20Bolt hole
processing 10 places

Detail of wooden beams
and hexagonal steel fittings

Perspective views   Frames of timber

PL-12 (SN400B)
Φ20Bolt

PL-35(SN490B)

Φ20Pin

Steel joint feathers Detail drawing 1:10

Roof structure construction detail

PRIMARY SCHOOL IN CROATIA

RANDIC TURATO

Location: Town of Krk, Island of Krk, Croatia
Photos: © Robert Les

Site plan

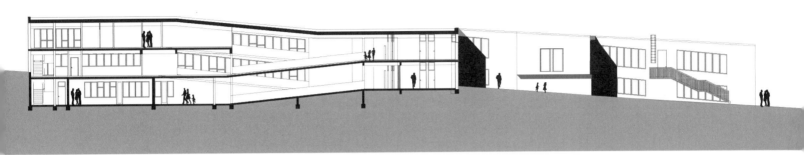

Section A

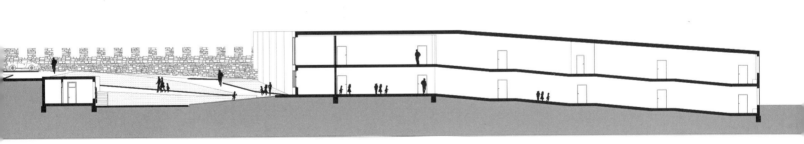

Section B

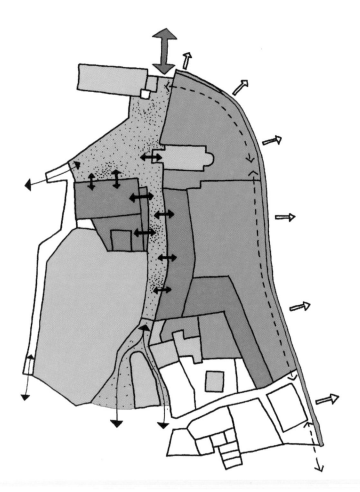

Sketches

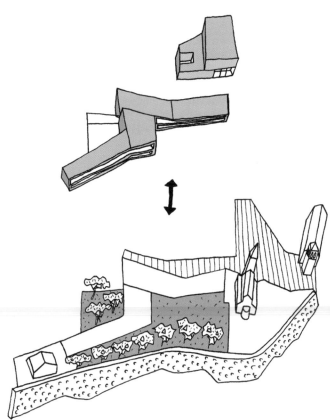

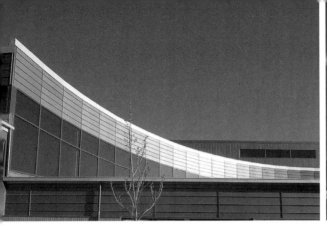

CLACKAMAS HIGH SCHOOL

BOORA ARCHITECTS
Location: Clackamas, Oregon, USA
Photos: © Michael Mathers

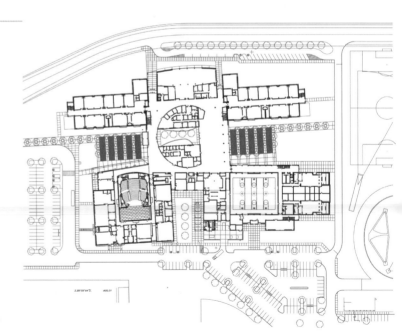

Site plan

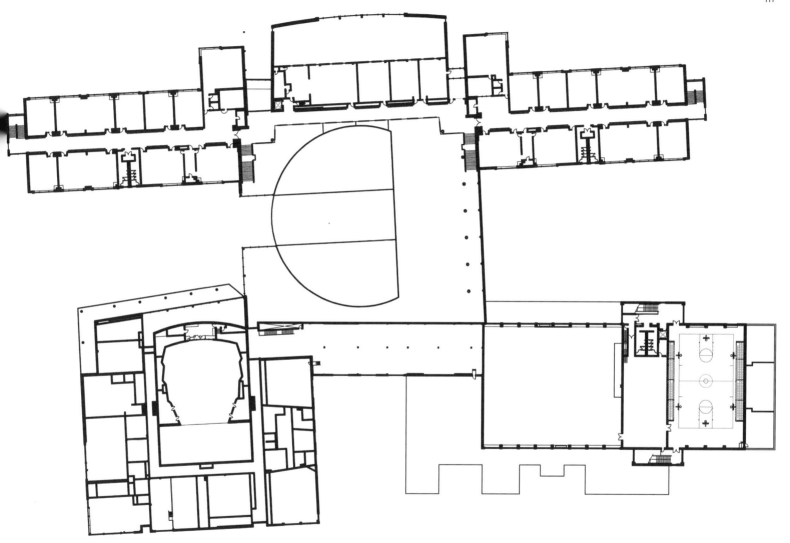

Main floor plan

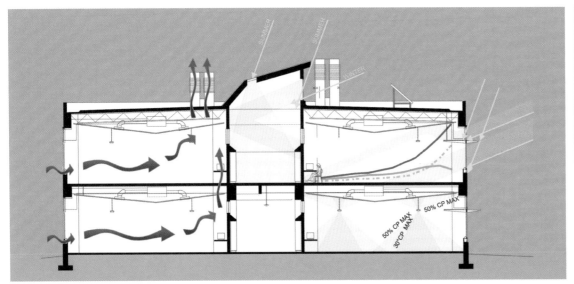

Light and ventilation inputs

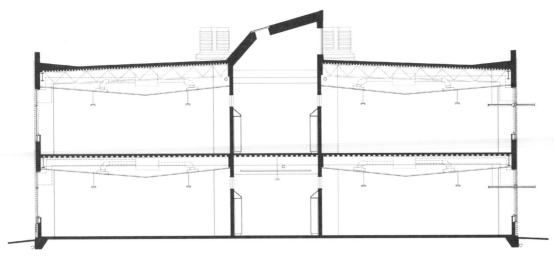

Section

KINDERGARTEN IN PEDEROBBA

C + S ASSOCIATI

Location: Pederobba, Italy
Photos: © Alessandra Chemollo, Carlo Cappai

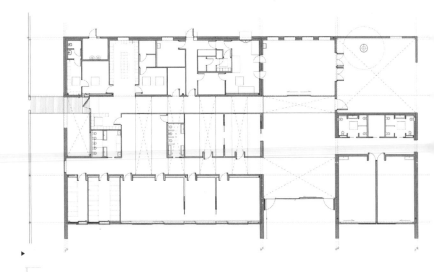

Main floor plan

Sections

Sections

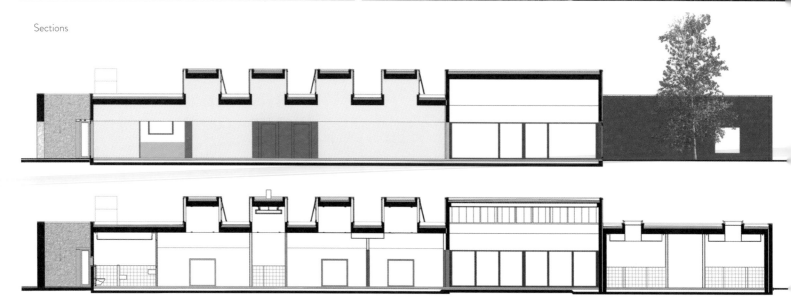

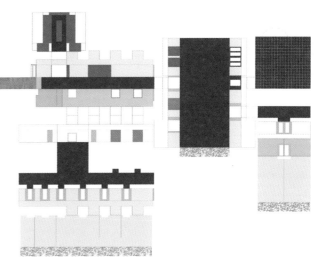

Dissection plan

Interior door/window
For children to 12-15 months

For children to 20-23 months

Exterior window north
For children to 30-36 months

Exterior door/window south
For children to 5 years

Colors help children to locate themselves.
Large windows provide natural light during the day.

WESTERN HOUSE ELEMENTARY SCHOOL

ADP ARCHITECTS
Location: Cippenham, UK
Photos: © Jonathan Moore

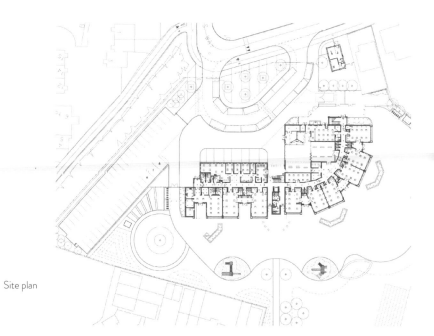

Site plan

North elevation

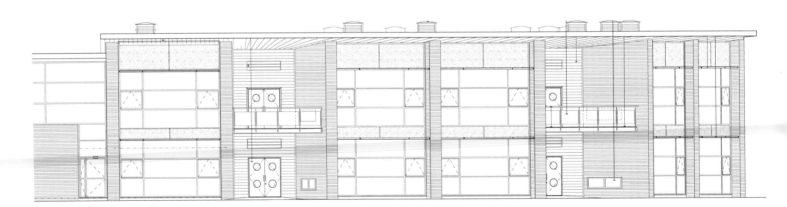

South elevation

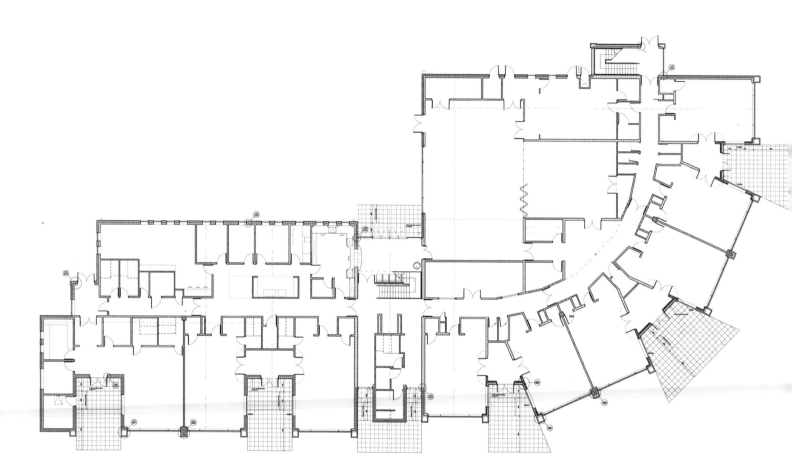

Ground floor

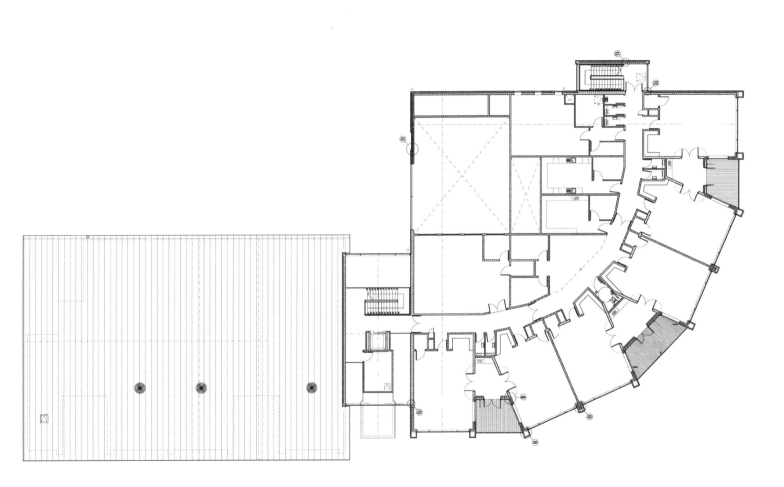

First floor

West Section

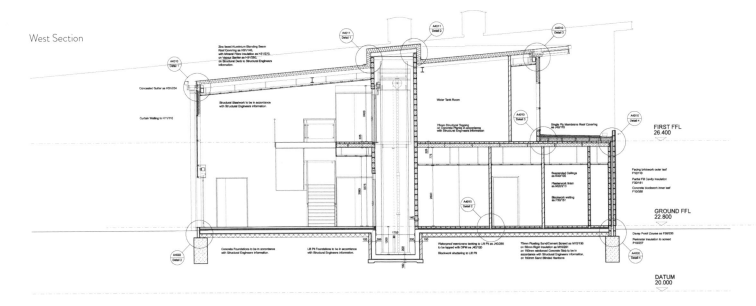

Zinc faced Aluminium Standing Seam
Roof Covering as H91/140,
with Mineral Fibre Insulation as H31/270,
on Vapour Barrier as H31/050,
on Structural Deck to Structural Engineers
information.

Concealed Gutter as H31/234

Structural Steelwork to be in accordance
with Structural Engineers information

Curtain Walling to H11/110

Water Tank Room

75mm Structural Topping
on Concrete Planks in accordance
with Structural Engineers information

Single Ply Membrane Roof Covering
as J42/170

FIRST FFL
26.400

Facing brickwork outer leaf
F10/110

Suspended Ceilings
as K40/105

Partial Fill Cavity Insulation
F30/161

Plasterwork finish
as M20/210

Concrete blockwork inner leaf
F10/350

Blockwork walling
as F30/151

GROUND FFL
22.800

Concrete Foundations to be in accordance
with Structural Engineers information.

Lift Pit Foundations to be in accordance
with Structural Engineers information.

Waterproof membrane tanking to Lift Pit
to be lapped with DPM as J40/285

Blockwork shuttering to Lift Pit

Damp Proof Course as F30/300

Perimeter insulation to screed
P10/257

75mm Floating Sand/Cement Screed as M10/130
on 50mm Rigid Insulation as M10/291
on 150mm reinforced Concrete Slab to be in
accordance with Structural Engineers information,
on 150mm Sand Blinded Hardcore

DATUM
20.000

MINAMI YAMASHIRO ELEMENTARY SCHOOL

RICHARD ROGERS PARTNERSHIP

Location: Kyoto, Japan

Photos: © Katsuhisa Kida

Front elevation plan

Ground floor

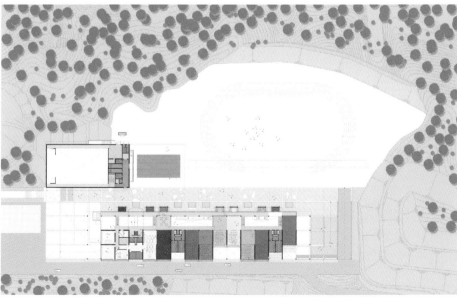

First floor

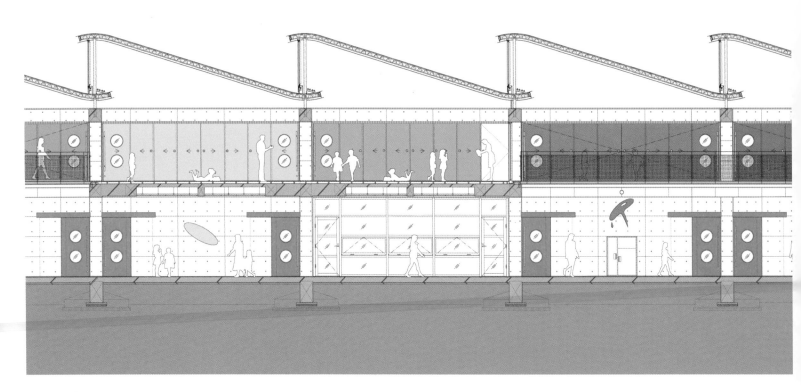

Section A

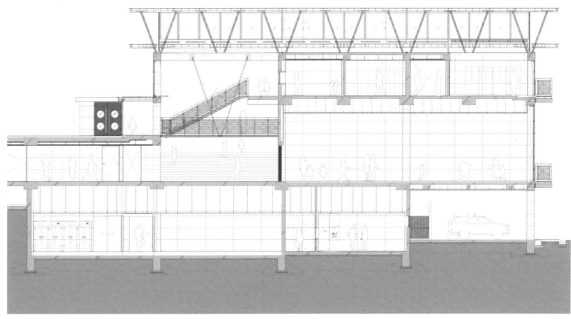

Section B

RINGSTABEKK HIGH SCHOOL

DIV. A ARKITEKTER

Location: Baerum, Norway

Photos: © Div. A Arkitekter, Hugo & Åshild

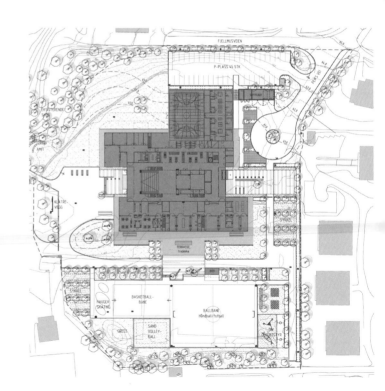

Site plan

East elevation

West elevation

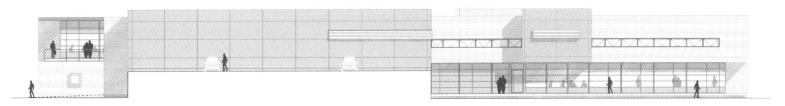

North elevation

South elevation

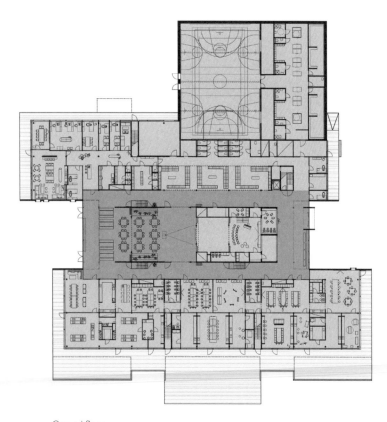

Ground floor

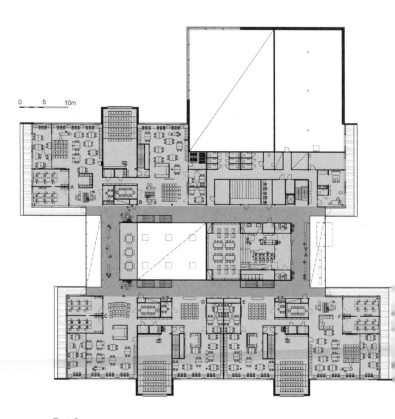

0   5   10m

First floor

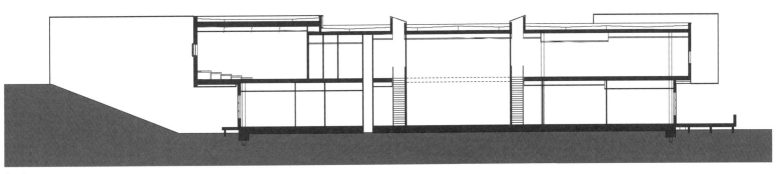

Section

ZAMET CENTER

3LHD ARCHITECTS

Location: Zamet, Croatia
Photos: © Domagoj Blažević, Damir Fabijanić, 3LHD archive

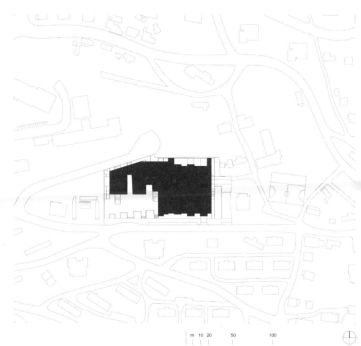

Site plan

m 10 20   50   100

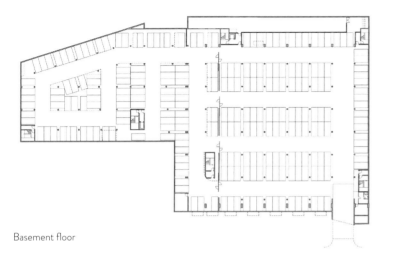

Basement floor

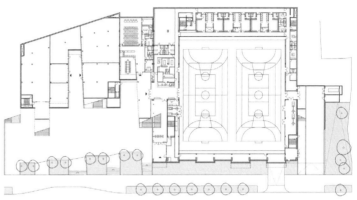

Ground floor plan

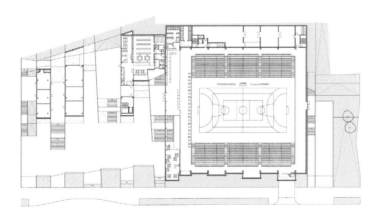

First floor plan

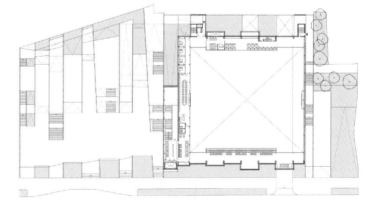

Second floor plan

Roof plan

m   10   20   50
| | | |

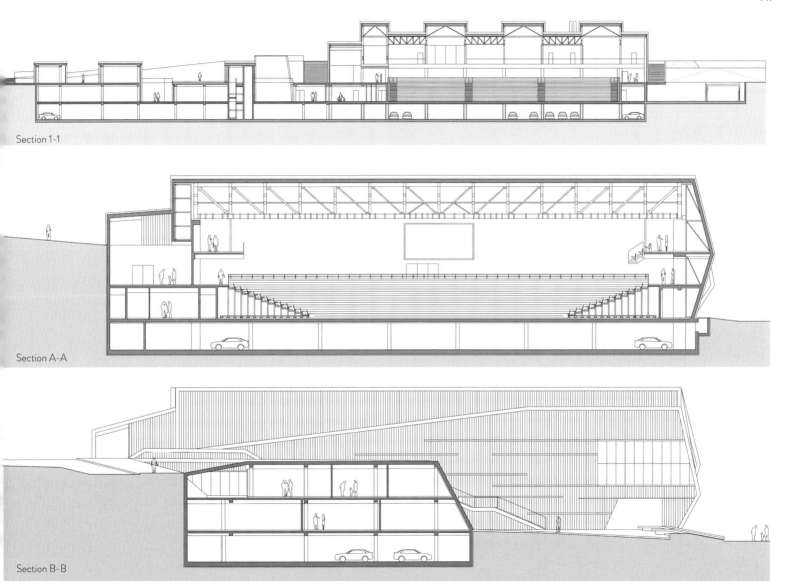

Section 1-1

Section A-A

Section B-B

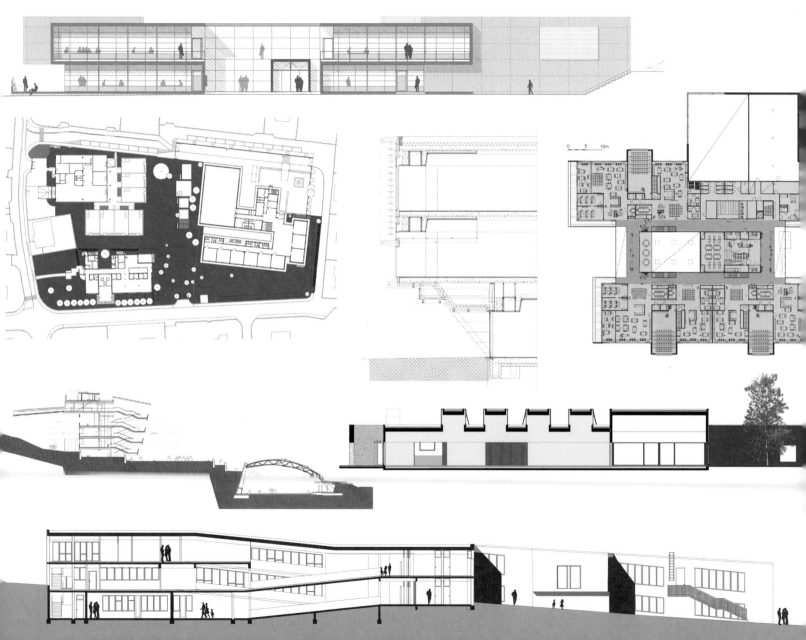